I UNDERSTAND....

# HEALTH
# INSURANCE

## BY RASHAWN WRIGHT

ADONAI PUBLISHING

CHICAGO

http://adonaipublishing.com

I Understand Health Insurance

Copyright © 2014 Rashawn Wright

Published By Adonai Publishing, Chicago, IL
November 2014

Adonai Publishing
http://adonaipublishing.com
rrh@adonaipublishing.com

ISBN-13: 978-1503120914
ISBN-10: 1503120910

# TABLE OF CONTENTS

# The Why

The Affordable Care Act has made it mandatory that everyone have health insurance, but most of us have no idea how health insurance actually works.

Being in the health care industry, I have encountered situations where people assume doctors are in-network with their health insurance plan, only after they receive a huge bill do they discover that the doctor is out-of network.

People have thought certain medical procedures were covered by their plan, but after the procedures are performed they receive a letter from their health insurance plan saying they have no benefits for that treatment. Again the person is stuck with a huge bill.

Situations like this are avoidable, but because we don't know the right questions to ask or who actually has the correct information, these situations are all too common.

The purpose of this book is to supply you with a basic understanding of health insurance and the most important things you should know. The information provided in this book will make you feel more confident as you choose and use your health insurance plan.

Let's Get Started!

## Affordable Care Act

The Affordable Care Act (ACA) is a law that attempts to reform U.S. Health Care by giving more Americans access to quality, affordable

> The Affordable Care Act is commonly referred to as Obamacare.

health insurance and by requiring coverage of preventive services.

## PRE – EXISTING CONDITION LIMITATIONS (PCL) –Insurance cannot deny coverage or charge higher premiums for those with existing medical conditions.

---

### WHAT COUNTS AS PREVENTIVE CARE?

**Wellness Visits & Physicals**
**Mammogram**
**Colonoscopy Screening**
**Prostate Cancer Screening**
**Blood Pressure and Cholesterol Screenings**
**Diabetes and STD Screenings**
**Routine vaccinations:**
  Hepatitis A and B
  Herpes Zoster
  Human Papillomavirus
  Influenza
  Measles, Mumps, Rubella
  Meningococcal
  Pneumococcal (pneumonia)
  Tetanus, Diphtheria, Pertussis (Whooping Cough)
  Varicella (chickenpox)

*Contact your insurance plan to find out what else is considered preventive.*

---

**PREVENTIVE CARE**- requires coverage of preventive care services and immunizations at no out of pocket cost for the insured if performed by in-network health care professionals, for health plans that start after 2014 and are not **grandfathered**. These services include some of the most important types of prevention like routine immunizations, mammograms and wellness visits.

> **GRANDFATHERED PLANS**
> Plans purchased before 3/23/2010 - these plans don't have to follow the Affordable Care Act.

**ESSENTIAL HEALTH BENEFITS** – Starting January 1st of 2014, the following "Essential Benefits" had to be included under all individual and small group health insurance plans with no lifetime or annual dollar limits:

- Emergency services
- Hospitalizations
- Laboratory services
- Maternity and Newborn care

> **Small Group Health Plans are insurance plans offered by employers who have 50 or less full time employees.**

9

- Mental health and substance abuse treatment
- Outpatient, or ambulatory care
- Pediatric care
- Prescription drugs
- Preventive care
- Rehabilitative and rehabilitative (helping maintain daily functioning) services
- Vision and dental care for children

**Exceptions:**

Insurance companies can still put a yearly dollar limit and a lifetime dollar limit on spending for health care services that are not considered essential health benefits, such as weight loss surgery and infertility services. Once that limit is reached, the

> **ANNUAL AND LIFETIME LIMITS**
> Health insurance companies sometimes have a maximum dollar amount cap on the benefits they will pay in a year or a lifetime when you're enrolled in a particular plan. Once that limit is reached the health plan will no longer pay for those benefits.

insured individual is responsible for paying the remaining expenses for those services.

## What if I don't get insurance?

By May 1st 2014 all non-exempt Americans will have to be enrolled in a type of health insurance known as minimum essential coverage, get an exemption, or face a tax penalty for each month they go without coverage.

*To find out more about the Affordable Care Act and what it means for you visit – http://www.healthcare.gov*

# Health Insurance

Health insurance is a contract that requires the insurance plan to pay some or all of your health care costs in exchange for a payment or **premium**.

Health insurance can be obtained through your employer or you can obtain your own plan through a licensed insurance broker, the health marketplace or through the government.

## Individual Health Plan

An **individual health plan** is insurance that you purchase for yourself and your family from a wide range of options through either the health marketplace or through a licensed insurance broker. With an individual plan you can choose the plan that has the best benefits for your lifestyle. You are responsible for the cost of the premium.

# Group Health Plan

A **group health plan** is insurance that you get through your place of employment or employment organization (union), which provides health benefits to you and your family. You share the cost of the premium with your employer. Your employer may offer you different plan options where the deductibles, out of pockets, or co-pays vary, but the services that are covered are largely the same. These plans will cover the essential health benefits mentioned previously and some may cover services like infertility procedures, weight loss treatments, acupuncture, or massage therapy.

# Medicare

Medicare is health insurance for persons over 65 and certain persons under 65 who are receiving Social Security disability benefits. It is administered by the US Department of Health and Human Services.

# Medicaid

Medicaid is health insurance for low or no income people who meet certain other requirements. These programs are administered by individual states.

# More Than One Insurance

These four ways to be insured are the most common. And it is possible to be insured by more than one type of plan at a time. For instance if you are actively employed and over the age of 65 you may have insurance through your employer as well as Medicare. Or if you and your spouse are both actively employed you may be covered by your own health plan and also covered by the plan of your spouse as a dependent. The children of actively employed parents can also be covered as dependents on the health plans of both parents.

If you have insurance through more than one source, each form of insurance can be used to pay for the allowed medical expenses. You just show the health care professional each insurance card for each health plan you have. The health care professional may ask you which plan is primary – that just means which insurance plan pays first. Determining how each insurance will pay for the medical care is called **coordination of benefits**.

Unfortunately, you can't just decide which insurance you want to be the primary. There are certain rules that insurance companies use to decide which insurance pays first. For instance, whichever plan is offered under your active employer is usually the primary plan. Or in the case of the child of actively employed parents, whichever parent's birthday comes first in the year is the primary for the child, unless a court order decrees that a particular parent's insurance is primary.

For example, if little Suzy's parents are divorced, and mommy's birthday is March 3$^{rd}$ and daddy's birthday is June 6$^{th}$, then mommy's health insurance pays first. But if the divorce decree says that daddy's plan is primary then Daddy's insurance will pay first.

There are several other rules that determine which insurance will be primary for various circumstances, if you are in any doubt just ask your insurance company.

If you have more than one health insurance it is important to inform each health insurance plan that you have another insurance. Why? Because if more than one insurance company pays as primary the health care professional can be overpaid, and if one of those insurance companies finds out that they have paid more money than they had to, they can ask you or your health care professional for a refund. It doesn't matter how much time has passed since the medical care was received or if you no longer have that insurance.

# How Do I Get Insurance

We looked at the various ways to be insured, and now we will examine how to get insurance. The ways you obtain insurance differ depending on where the insurance comes from.

If your employer offers insurance, the first time you are eligible for insurance is when you are initially hired. If you are interested in individual insurance, contact an insurance broker to find out when you are eligible. If you think you qualify for Medicaid,

---

**MEDICARE: WHEN AM I ELIGIBLE?**

If you are age 65 or older, or

If you have been entitled to Social Security disability benefits for at least 24 months, or

If you have End Stage Renal Disease, or

If you have Lou Gehrig's Disease

---

contact your state's Medicaid program. If you think you qualify for Medicare, contact your local Social Security office.

## Eligibility

**Eligibility** basically determines who is qualified for insurance by specific health plans. If you have insurance through your employer or if you buy an individual plan you are considered the **policyholder**. Most insurance plans also allow dependents. The main types of dependents are the spouse and children of the policyholder.

Before choosing a health plan, you must ask your employer or insurance broker who will be considered a dependent on your plan. Some plans offer coverage for domestic partners, adult dependents, disabled dependents, and grandchildren.

# Changing Insurance

Let's say you already have insurance through your employer, but they offer a different type of plan, and you would like that plan instead of the one you have, or you don't like any of the plans the employer offers and you want to get an individual plan. The only time you will be able to change your plan is during **open enrollment** period.

Open enrollment is a period of time during each year when you can enroll in a health plan or make changes. The dates of open enrollment depend on who is offering the insurance plan. If it is through your employer, then the employer will inform you of the dates. If you want to get an individual plan, then ask the insurance broker when open enrollment is.

Of course, there are exceptions to this. Let's say you just had a baby and need to add the baby to your insurance plan, but open enrollment is 6 months away. In the meantime, you want to take your baby for well check visits, how do you get insurance for your baby? Besides, the new hire period, the only time you can obtain insurance, change insurance, or add dependents outside of open enrollment is if you have had a qualifying **life event**.

There are very specific occasions that are considered qualifying life events: marriage, divorce, having a baby, adoption, moving to a new state, gain or loss of coverage, or loss of income. If you have a qualifying life event contact your employer or insurance broker soon after the event because there are time requirements for making these changes.

---

**ASK MY EMPLOYER**

**Employers generally have a Human Resource Department (HR) or Benefit Center that can answer certain questions about the benefits the employer offers. In this text when we say ask your employer, we are referring to the HR department or the Benefit Center.**

---

Ask your employer or insurance broker if there are other events that may be considered a qualifying life event for your health insurance plan.

## Losing Insurance

You can lose health insurance if your employment status changes or if you stop paying your individual insurance plan premiums. If you stop paying premiums because of a change in income, you may be eligible for other types of insurance like Medicaid, or your insurance broker may know of a lower cost plan that may fit your needs.

If you lose your job, or no longer have full time hours, but would like to continue with the same insurance that is offered by the employer, you may be eligible for **COBRA**.

# Consolidated Omnibus Budget Reconciliation Act (COBRA)

COBRA gives employees and their dependents who lose their health insurance the right to choose to continue the insurance provided by their group health plan for a limited time. Group insurance can be lost due to voluntary or involuntary job loss, reduction in the hours worked, transition between jobs, death, divorce, and other life events. You may be required to pay the entire premium for the health plan.

COBRA basically extends the insurance coverage that is obtained through an employer even though a person no longer works for that employer, or is otherwise ineligible according to the requirements of the employer, for instance, no longer a full time employee, but now part time, etc.

Earlier we mentioned that employers share the cost of the premium with the employee. Well, if a person becomes eligible for COBRA, most of the time the employer no longer shares the cost, so the premium for a person on COBRA is much higher than what they originally paid through their employer. The amount of time that a person or their dependents can remain on COBRA is limited, ask your employer for more information about COBRA.

# Types of Insurance Plans

Now that you know the ways you can get insurance, it's time to talk about the different health plan types. There are two main plan types, with each offering different variations on the major components of the health plans. Loosely speaking, the two types are **HMO** and **PPO**. Have you ever called a doctor's office to set up an appointment and they asked, "Do you have an HMO or PPO?" and you have no idea what they are talking about. You look at your insurance card, and don't see either acronym on the card – well now you can find out what they mean.

## HMO

HMO stands for Health Maintenance Organization. **The major difference between this plan type and the PPO is that it is considered physician directed.** That means it requires the member to have a primary care physician (PCP) who basically directs the health care of the member.

HMOs can also require the member to have a referral from their primary care physician before they see a specialist for any other condition. For example, if the member is having an issue with their eyes they can't just go to an ophthalmologist, they have to first schedule a visit with their primary care physician, who will then examine the member and refer the member to an ophthalmologist. The specialist recommended is usually part of the same medical group as the primary care physician, since HMOs rarely have out of network benefits.

There are various subcategories for HMOs that offer slight variations, like allowing out of network benefits, or

> Point of Service or POS plans are like HMOs but they also have out-of-network benefits.

waiving the referral requirement for specialists' visits.

Contact your insurance company for information about the type of plan you have.

With so many restrictions, why would anyone choose this plan – because of copays. HMOs generally require the members to only pay a copay instead of meeting a deductible for doctor's office visits, urgent care visits, surgeries, or laboratory services. A copay is usually a much smaller amount than a deductible.

# PPO

PPO stands for Preferred Provider Organization. **These plans are considered self-directed or consumer driven**. You can see a specialist without prior referrals. You don't have to choose a primary care physician, and you generally have in and out-of-network benefits which may vary. PPOs can also have deductibles and an out of pocket maximum per plan year.

PPOs may have a copay for office visits, urgent care, or ER visits, but some of them have no copays at all and the member must meet a deductible before the insurance plan pays any amount towards the cost of medical procedures. Once this deductible is met, the member may be required to split the cost of treatment with the insurance plan until the out of pocket maximum is met. When the out of pocket is met, that is when the insurance plan will pay 100% of the eligible cost for the treatment.

PPOs also have various subtypes that can offer a different network of doctors to use, or no network at all – which means you can see any doctor for the exact same benefits. The plan that doesn't use a network of doctors offers the most freedom and can be called an Indemnity plan, Comprehensive plan, Major Medical plan, or Base plan depending on the insurance company.

Since PPOs can have some relatively high deductibles (some can number in the thousands of dollars) there are some add-ons that can be offered to help with the cost of those high deductibles. These add-ons are called HRAs, HSAs, and FSAs.

## HEALTH REIMBURSEMENT ACCOUNT (HRA)

The HRA is an employer funded account that is used to pay 100% of eligible out of pocket medical expenses until the account is empty. This means that funds from the HRA can be used to pay the deductible, copay, or coinsurance that the employee or their dependent is responsible for.

The funds generally don't roll over from year to year – but some employers will allow this. The only things that an HRA can be used to pay for are benefits that are actually allowed by the medical plan. For example, if your health plan does not have coverage for Acupuncture you cannot use your HRA to pay for it. The HRA, normally, does not have a debit card or checks attached to it – the insurance plan administers the payment of the HRA to the eligible claims.

## HEALTH SAVINGS ACCOUNT (HSA)

An HSA is a tax advantaged savings account that can be used to pay for qualified health care costs. The amount that will be contributed to the HSA is decided at the beginning of the plan year, but that total amount is not available until the end of the calendar year. The account is funded by the employer, the employee, or both as the plan year progresses. This means that money is added to the account at each pay period until it is funded completely for the year.

The funds in this account can be used any year, not just one plan year. The HSA usually has a debit card that the member receives at the beginning of the plan year, and for additional fees, checks can also be used to pay eligible expenses. The member can use the debit card or checks to pay for deductibles, copays, the cost of eye exams, contacts, or eyeglasses (which are generally not covered by a medical plan), or even some exercise equipment prescribed by a doctor.

The HSA can also be used to pay for some benefits that are not allowed by the insurance plan, like acupuncture, some restrictions or criteria may apply. For a full list of items that an HSA can be used to pay, contact your insurance plan.

**FLEXIBLE SPENDING ACCOUNT (FSA)**
A FSA allows employees to set aside pre-tax dollars to pay for certain health care or dependent care costs during a specific time period. Funds are deposited into the account each pay period from the employee's salary and any funds not spent at the end of the plan year are lost. Also there is a maximum amount that can be contributed each year.

# Who Pays What

## Premiums

The premium is the responsibility of the insured individual. It is a periodic payment that is required to keep the health insurance active. If you have health insurance through your place of employment, the part of the premium that you are responsible for is deducted from your paycheck. If you have purchased health insurance through an insurance broker, or online, you pay the premium to the insurance company.

## Copay

The **copay** is a fixed amount that the insured pays for a covered medical procedure at the time of the service. Usually if a procedure has a copay, that is all the insured individual has to pay before the insurance plan pays the rest of the allowed expenses for the procedure, but there are some procedures that have a copay as well as a deductible and/or coinsurance that the insured individual has to pay before the insurance plan pays anything for the procedure.

> **Copays usually apply to doctor's office visits, Emergency Room visits, Hospital inpatient stays, or Urgent Care visits, but some plans have copays for other procedures as well.**

## Deductible

The deductible is the amount per plan year that the member is required to pay before the insurance plan will pay anything towards eligible medical expenses.

The deductible resets every 12 months. This means that the amount you have contributed towards the deductible goes back to 0. The date of the reset depends on the type of **plan year** you have. A **calendar year** plan starts on January 1$^{st}$ and ends on December 31$^{st}$. A **contract year** plan is a 12 consecutive month period which start and end dates may be different from the calendar year. For instance, a contract year can be from July 1$^{st}$ to June 30$^{th}$, etc. Contact your insurance company to find out when your deductible starts over.

**High deductible Plans** are basically insurance plans with high deductibles. They can have deductibles of $2,500, $3,000, $7,000, $10,000, etc. These amounts must be paid before the insurance plan will pay anything. These plans sometimes have HRAs, HSAs, or FSAs attached to help offset some of the deductible cost.

# Individual and Family vs. Plan Deductible

The deductible can have various levels. The **individual deductible** is the amount that just one person on the plan has to meet before the insurance plan begins to pay for part or all of his/her eligible medical expenses. Let's say the Martin family of 3 have an insurance plan with an individual deductible of $500 and a family deductible of $1250. If one member of the family has to have a procedure done at the hospital, this means that he has to pay $500 dollars of the allowed expenses for the procedure before the insurance plan covers either part or all of the remaining allowed expenses.

The **family deductible** is the amount that all the individual deductibles contribute to. Once this amount is met everyone on the plan can now have the insurance plan begin to pay for part or all of the eligible medical expenses. For example, the Johnson family has 4 members all covered by one insurance plan. The plan has an individual deductible of $500 per calendar year and a family deductible of $1500 per calendar year. Each time a member of that family meets some part of his/her individual deductible, that amount is subtracted from the family deductible. This means that not everyone on the plan will be required to meet the entire individual deductible of $500.

For example, two family members can meet their entire $500 deductible and the other two would only be required to meet part of their $500 deductible before the entire $1500 family deductible is met.

No one on the plan can exceed their individual deductible in order to meet the entire family deductible. That means that if one member of the family has more medical expenses than others, that family member can only contribute his individual deductible to the family deductible.

If there is a **plan deductible,** then there is no individual deductible. The plan deductible is the amount that everyone on the plan contributes to before the insurance plan pays part or all of the eligible medical expenses for anyone on the plan. Let's say the Smith family of 6 has a plan deductible of $1850. Everyone on the health plan has to pay all of their allowed medical expenses until that $1850 is met.

This allows the person who may require more medical treatments to contribute a larger amount to the plan deductible instead of being limited by an individual deductible.

## Co-insurance

**Co-insurance** is a shared percentage between the insured and their health insurance plan for the allowed medical expenses. Usually coinsurance is not applied until the deductible has been met for the insured, but there are some plans that have no deductible for certain medical services, they just start off with a co-insurance.

As mentioned earlier co-insurance is usually expressed as a percentage, with the insurance plan paying the higher percentage of allowed medical expenses. So if an insurance plan has a co-insurance of 80/20. That means the insurance plan pays 80% of the allowed procedure while the insured individual pays only 20%.

So back to the Martin family: We mentioned they had an individual deductible of $500 and a family deductible of $1250, well after their deductible is met they have a coinsurance of 90/10. That means once one member of the family has met their individual deductible of $500, the insurance plan will start to pay 90% of the allowed expenses and the family member has to pay 10% of the medical expenses.

Another scenario: let's say 2 members of the Martin family have met their individual deductible of $500 and the third member, Cole, has to have a medical procedure but has not met his individual deductible yet. Remember we talked earlier about the individual deductible contributing to the family deductible. Since the other two members of the Martin family have met their $500 individual deductible that means that $1000 of the $1250 family deductible has been met.

So, if the allowed amount for Cole's Medical expenses is $750 – that means that Cole only has to pay $250 of his individual deductible before the Family deductible of $1250 is met.

Once that family deductible is met the plan's 90/10 coinsurance begins so the insurance plan will begin to pay 90% of Cole's allowed expenses and Cole only has to pay 10%.

So, of that $750 medical bill, Cole has to pay $250 to meet the family deductible and then only 10% of the remaining $500 *($750 - $250 = $500)* – which is $50 *($500 x 10% =$50)*. That means Cole pays $300 *($250 deductible + $50 coinsurance)* total for his medical procedure and his insurance plan pays $450 *($750 - $300 = $450)*.

## Out of Pocket

The **Out of Pocket** (OOP) is the most the insured individual pays during a plan year before the insurance plan begins to pay 100% of the allowed medical expenses. The OOP resets every 12 months. This means that the amount you have contributed towards the OOP goes back to 0. The date of the reset depends on the type of plan year you have.

The OOP can include the deductible, copays, and coinsurance that the insured individual is responsible for paying. That means that all of those amounts are added until they reach the OOP and then the insurance plan will pay all of the allowed expenses for medical procedures and the individual no longer has to pay for the allowed medical expenses.

There are some plans where the deductibles and/or copays do not contribute to the OOP. That means that only the percentage of the coinsurance that the insured pays will be added to meet the OOP. Plan premiums and non-covered expenses never contribute to the plan OOP.

## Individual and Family vs. Plan OOP

The OOP has different levels like the deductible. The **individual OOP** is the amount one person on the plan has to meet per plan year before the insurance plan pays 100% of the allowed medical expenses. The **family OOP** is the amount that all the individual OOPs contribute to per plan year before the insurance plan pays 100% of the allowed medical expenses for everyone on the plan.

The **Plan OOP** is the amount that all insured individuals on the plan contribute to per plan year before the insurance plan pays 100% of the allowed medical expenses for everyone on the plan. If the insurance plan has a plan OOP then there is no individual OOP – everyone on the plan must pay whatever their responsibility is of the allowed expenses until the plan OOP has been met.

# So What's Covered?

It's time to clear up a mass misconception. The term "**covered**" when referring to a medical procedure does not mean that the insurance plan will pay for the entire cost of the procedure. "Covered" just means that the insurance plan has benefits for that procedure – which can include a copay, deductible, or coinsurance that the insured individual is responsible for paying before the insurance plan will pay anything. You have to be very specific when it comes to finding out what and how something is covered by your insurance plan.

Now there are procedures that can be covered 100% by an insurance plan but there are usually specific requirements for these procedures. For example, the Affordable Care Act has made preventive care something that most insurance plans have to cover 100% of the cost, but the doctor's office or hospital usually has to be in network with your specific insurance plan and very specific codes have to be billed by the health care professional before the procedures are considered preventive.

**I THOUGHT IT WAS FREE!**

The billing codes and costs for a regular doctor's office visit and a preventive doctor's office visit are very different, and there are some doctors who will bill for both visits at the same time if you talk to that doctor about any health issues you may be having.

So, while you initially went in for your preventive visit which your insurance plan may cover 100% – you could receive a bill from the doctor's office for an office visit because when he asked how the arthritis was doing and you responded about your various health issues, that just became a regular office visit in addition to the preventive visit.

Maybe the doctor only said take some aspirin for that…or maybe only gave you a pamphlet to read – but that doctor can now bill you for a regular office visit, even though the main reason for the visit was for preventive care.

# Network

A network consists of the health care professionals, hospitals, surgical centers, suppliers, and labs that have a contract with your health insurance plan to provide medical services. Not all health care professionals want to deal with the rules and regulations that are required by being contracted with insurance companies. So, that is why health care professionals can have two different classifications when it comes to your insurance plan. Are they **in-network** or **out-of-network**? The answer to this question will determine what level of benefits will apply to your medical procedures by that particular health care professional.

## In-Network Benefits vs. Out of Network Benefits

An insurance plan can have different levels of benefits. These different levels are usually distinguished by the terms in-network and out-of-network. In-network benefits are usually much better than out-of network benefits. They can have lower deductibles, lower coinsurance responsibilities for the insured individual as well as copays.

If a health care professional is **in-network** then they have a contract with the insurance plan to be included in a particular network. The contracted health care professional can only accept a certain amount for covered medical procedures. This amount is called a **contracted rate**.

An in-network health care professional can charge anything they like for a medical procedure, but if the amount they bill is more than the contracted rate for that procedure, then they have to write-off the difference and cannot bill the patient or the insurance company for that amount. So if a doctor charges $200 for an office visit, but his contract with the insurance company says he can only be reimbursed for $50, then that extra $150 has to be considered a discount and the in-network doctor cannot bill the patient, or the patient's insurance company for that $150.

The in-network health care professionals typically submit the bill to the insurance company before they bill the patient, and if a person's insurance plan requires authorization for certain procedures it is the in-network health care professional's responsibility to get that authorization from the insurance company.

### AUTHORIZATION

**Some medical treatments require authorization or precertification before an insurance company will allow coverage for them. Authorization is basically proving that a treatment or procedure is medical necessary according to the requirements of the insurance company. If authorization is denied by the insurance company but you have the procedure done, you will be responsible for the entire cost of the procedure.**

# Out-of-Network

Health care professionals who don't have a contract with a specific health plan are considered out-of-network. Not all insurance plans have out-of-network benefits. That means that if you see a doctor or go to a hospital that is not part of your insurance plan's network – you will be responsible for the costs, the insurance plan will not pay for any of it. There may be some exceptions to this – ask your insurance plan's customer service department.

If an insurance plan does have out-of-network benefits, most of the time, they are not as good as the in-network benefits. The deductibles and coinsurance can be much higher. And there is no contracted rate that the health care professionals have to accept. There is a **maximum reimbursable charge** that the insurance plan may consider an appropriate cost for procedures, but that may be much less than what the health care professional has actually billed.

The maximum reimbursable charge is also known as usual and customary charge; it is based on the average charges for that procedure in a specific geographical region. Remember, the health care professionals can charge whatever amount they like for procedures, but if that health care professional is out-of-network they do not have to write off or discount any amount that the insurance company considers acceptable. If the insurance company does not allow all of the charges that the out of network health care professional bills – the customer can and most of the time is held responsible for paying the difference.

For example, let's take that same doctor's office visit we talked about earlier. If the doctor charges $200 for the visit, but the maximum reimbursable rate is only $50 then the insurance plan will only apply $50 to the individual's benefits. That means that the doctor can bill the member for the

$150 that is not an allowed medical expense, and none of that $150 will be applied towards the deductible, or out of pocket, or copays for the plan.

Out of network healthcare professionals can also refuse to submit the bills to the insurance company, or to request authorization for certain procedures. The customer can be made to pay for the entire cost of the service and seek reimbursement from their insurance company later. **Sometimes out of network health care professionals don't even use medical codes on their bills – which makes it virtually impossible for the customer to get reimbursed by their insurance company.**

## Common Benefits

So let's talk about the actual benefits or covered services. Covered services are the procedures that the insurance plan allows "coverage" for. Earlier we mentioned that covered does not mean that the insurance plan pays for the entire procedure, it just means that the plan has benefits for that procedure. Which means that the benefit for a particular procedure may apply to the customer's deductible, coinsurance, or a copay amount.

Your plan booklet or summary usually tells what procedures are covered and how they will be covered. You can also call the insurance plan's customer service department to find out this information. The customer service phone number is usually on the back of your insurance card.

The Affordable Care Act requires individual and small group insurance plans to offer in-network benefits for certain services that are considered essential. These essential health benefits are:

**EMERGENCY SERVICES** – that includes ambulance services to the Emergency Room, the Emergency Room, the tests done in the Emergency Room and the doctors that were seen in the Emergency Room.

Contact your insurance plan to find out exactly how these services are covered.

**HOSPITALIZATION** – This is when a health care professional has determined it is necessary that a person stays in the hospital overnight, or for a number of days. Most insurance plans require the hospital or doctor that is recommending the inpatient stay to get authorization first. The insurance plan has its own medical directors in specific fields that can review the medical records and notes provided by the hospital or doctor and decide whether an inpatient stay is medically necessary. If authorized, the insurance plan will allow the charges. If not authorized, the charges will be denied.

**LABORATORY SERVICES** – bloodwork or tissue samples that are necessary for determining health issues. Again some lab procedures require authorization.

**MATERNITY AND NEWBORN CARE** - This is coverage for pregnancy and the delivered baby. Coverage is only available for eligible dependents, the spouse on the plan or main policyholder. Plans rarely allow grandchildren to be a dependent on an insurance plan, and sometimes if a daughter on the insurance plan is pregnant – maternity benefits are only available if there are complications with the pregnancy. Contact your insurance company to find out more.

**MENTAL HEALTH AND SUBSTANCE ABUSE** – This is coverage for seeing a therapist, psychologist, psychiatrist, licensed counsellor, and for rehab facilities. Remember, inpatient stays may require authorization from the insurance plan.

**OUTPATIENT OR AMBULATORY CARE** – This includes medically necessary surgeries or procedures performed in hospital outpatient areas or surgical centers. Sometimes authorization is required, so contact your insurance plan before surgical procedures. This also includes visits to your doctor's office or specialist office visits – like a Dermatologist, Ear, Nose, and Throat doctor, etc.

**PEDIATRIC CARE** – This includes doctor's office visits for children who are dependents on the insurance plan– these services may be subject to a copay or deductible.

**PREVENTIVE AND WELLNESS CARE** – Annual physicals, well care visits, immunizations. Contact your insurance plan to find out exactly what is considered preventive. The Affordable Care Act has made it mandatory for most insurance plans to cover the entire cost of preventive care – that means no copay, no deductible, and no patient responsibility. But for most plans, the health care professional has to be in network and has to bill with the specific medical codes that are considered preventive codes.

**REHABILITATIVE CARE AND SERVICES AND DEVICES** – This is physical therapy, speech therapy, chiropractic therapy, occupational therapy, artificial limbs, and other medical equipment, etc., basically services that help maintain daily functions. Some therapies or devices require medical necessity review and there is sometimes a limit to the number of therapy days per year. Contact your insurance plan to find out the limits and what services and equipment are actually covered.

Some insurance plans only cover these essential benefits if the services are provided by an in network health care professional. Contact your insurance plan to find out how these benefits are covered.

There are insurance plans that also cover acupuncture, massage therapy, bariatric surgery (weight loss surgery), prosthetic or orthotic devices, infertility services, breast reduction surgery.

If your insurance plan covers these services there may be authorization required or special criteria that has to be met before the procedure will be covered. Contact your insurance plan to find out what is covered, when it's covered, and how it is covered.

---

### WHO DETERMINES BENEFITS?

Have you talked to friends and found out that their insurance offers benefits for procedures like massage therapy, acupuncture, or bariatric surgery – and yours doesn't? Why is that? Well, it depends on who you have insurance through.

If you have insurance through your employer then your employer determines what benefits are offered on your insurance plan.

If you have an individual plan your benefits are limited by the types of plans offered by the insurance company.

---

# The Money!

## Claims

A **claim** is a payment request to the insurance plan for medical services that have already been provided. A claim can be submitted by the health care professional, the patient, or the patient's representative.

## The In Network Process

If the health care professional is in network, they are responsible for submitting the claim to the insurance plan. All you have to do is provide the health care professional or facility with your insurance card information.

# The Out of Network Process

If the health care professional is out of network, they might not submit claims to the insurance company. That health care professional may give the patient an itemized bill and then it is the patient's responsibility to submit the claim to the insurance company to get reimbursed for the services.

If your health care professional is out of network – it helps to ask if they will submit the claim to your insurance company. Some health care professionals may say no because they just don't want to deal with insurance companies. If the answer is no there are some things that you are going to need from the doctor in order to submit the claim yourself.

**You will need an itemized statement.**

This statement should have the health care professional's name and address, their tax id number, a line by line breakdown of each procedure code and their separate prices, and the diagnosis code that gives the reason why you needed the procedures.

If you have out of network benefits the itemized statement is the most important thing you are going to need in order to be reimbursed by your health plan. Always make a copy of this statement and only send the copies to the insurance company. Keep your originals for your own records.

**You will need a receipt.**

If an HCP is out of network you may have to pay for the treatment before you leave. If this is the case make sure you get a receipt for this payment.

**You will need a claim form.**

Most insurance companies have claim forms that you need to fill out if you are submitting the claim yourself. Ask your insurance company where you can get the claim reimbursement form. You fill out this form and submit it with your itemized statement and receipt to your insurance company.

If you have to submit your own claim, make sure you do so as soon as possible, because there are time requirements that have to be met in order for your claims to be processed.

## Timely Filing

The claim has to be submitted to the insurance plan before a certain amount of time. This time may vary by state but the norm is usually 90 days for an in-network doctor or 180 days for a facility (hospital or surgical center, etc.), or an out-of-network doctor. This means the in network doctor has until 90 days after the **date of service** (the day you went to see the doctor) to send the claim to the insurance plan. Facility claims or claims for out of network doctors have to be submitted before 180 days have passed. This is considered **timely filing**.

Again the timely filing requirements may vary by state and/or insurance plan so contact your insurance plan to find out the requirements. If a claim is not filed within that time frame then it will be denied by the insurance plan. If this happens and the claim is from an in network health care professional, the contract that they have with the insurance plan does not allow them to bill the patient. If an out of network claim is denied for timely filing then the patient is responsible for paying the full cost.

## Claim Status

Once the claims are submitted they are processed by computers or a claim processor. Claims can take several days to process once they are received. This time frame varies by insurance company. If a claim is taking longer to process than stated by the insurance company then it will be pended.

# Pended Claims

A claim can be pended if the insurance plan needs more information from the health care professional, such as, medical records or information about the health care professional, such as, the tax id number or a copy of the medical license. A claim can be pended if certain information is missing from the claim form or if the information is incorrect – such as, medical billing codes.

A claim can also be pended if the patient has more than one insurance plan and the secondary insurance plan needs information from the primary insurance plan or if a plan has pre-existing condition limitations and the insurance plan needs verification that the claim is not for a pre-existing condition.

If more information is needed the insurance plan contacts the health care professional asking for that specific information.  The insurance plan will also inform the member that additional information has been requested from the health care professional.

A claim can also be pended for internal reasons. These reasons can include very large charge amounts that require additional review to verify the pricing for the particular medical procedure. If the claim is pended internally contact your insurance plan to find out how much longer it will take to be processed.

## Processed Claims

Once the claim is processed the patient will receive an **explanation of benefits (EOB)** that tells how the claim was processed, what the insurance plan paid, what the patient is responsible for paying. It also includes details such as the date of service, the doctor or facility name, the type of procedure performed, whether the doctor or facility is in network or out of network.

The EOB may also tell how much has been applied towards the deductibles and out-of-pocket for the plan year. The EOB is not a bill; it is just a record of that specific medical procedure and a guide to make sure that the patient is billed correctly by the health care professional.

The health care professional also receives a similar statement from the insurance plan. This statement is called an **explanation of payment (EOP)** and if the insurance plan is responsible for paying the health care professional any amount for that particular claim, the EOP may also include a check or electronic check information. If the healthcare professional is in network this is how they know what to bill the patient. If the health care professional sends you a bill for more than your EOB says you owe, contact the insurance plan.

# Denials

Sometimes all or part of a claim is denied. This means that the services are not covered by the insurance plan. This can happen if the insurance plan receives two of the exact same claims from a health care professional. One claim will be denied as a duplicate and the other processed correctly. A claim can be denied if there are no benefits for a particular procedure. Some plans don't have benefits for acupuncture so if you or your acupuncturist submits a claim it will be denied.

If a procedure required preauthorization but the health care professional did not get the authorization the claim will be denied. If a health care professional is out of network and the insurance plan does not have out of network benefits, that claim will be denied. A claim can be denied for timely filing if it is not filed on time. A claim can be denied if a person is no longer covered by the insurance plan – because they did not pay the premium or they are no longer employed by the company they had insurance through.

A claim can be denied if the insurance plan never received the additional information that was requested from the health care professional. Your explanation of benefits will usually tell you why your claim was denied. Contact your insurance plan for more information or to request an adjustment if you feel the claim was denied in error.

## Adjustments

Insurance plans receive millions of claims, all of which have to be processed according to a specific timeframe. With this type of pressure it is not unheard of for mistakes to be made when the claims are being processed.

When a claim is processed incorrectly there is a procedure for getting the claim corrected. This correction process is considered an **adjustment**.

Some common mistakes can include the claim being processed with out-of-network benefits for an in-network health care professional, the deductible being applied when the benefit says a copay should apply, or a patient responsibility when the medical procedure should be covered 100% by the insurance plan.

It is important to look at your EOB because this is the easiest way for you to find out if a mistake has been made. If you think a mistake has been made, then call your insurance plan immediately because you only have a certain amount of time to request an adjustment. This timeframe may vary depending on your insurance plan and whether your health care professional is in network or out of network.

# Appeals

If your claim, or adjustment request, or authorization for a procedure is denied and you feel it was denied in error, you or your health care professional can file an appeal. An appeal is a request for the insurance plan to review a claim or decision again.

Filing an appeal does not guarantee that the initial decision will be changed. Some insurance plans have specific requirements for filing an appeal. They may have to be filed within a certain timeframe, or sent to a specific address, or have specific forms that need to be filled out or included. Contact your insurance plan to find out these requirements.

# Questions, Questions

In order to get the most out of your health insurance there are certain questions you need to ask. This section will focus on those questions and who you ask for the most accurate answer.

## Things to ask my employer or insurance broker...

How can I add dependents to my plan?

When can I change my insurance plan?

When is open enrollment?

Why is my insurance plan terminated?

Can I add benefits for acupuncture, massage, bariatric surgery, etc., to my plan?

What's my premium?

If my spouse is offered insurance at work and he or she does not except it will my premium be more if I add my spouse to my plan?

## Things to ask your health care professional

What's my diagnosis code?

What's my procedure code?

---

### DIAGNOSIS CODE

The diagnosis code is the reason why the health care professional wants you to have the procedure. Diagnosis codes look like this: v70.00, 300.00, 723.9, v76.0, 274.9.

### PROCEDURE CODE

The procedure code is what the health care professional wants you to have done. Procedure codes can look like this: 92213 (office visit), L3000 (foot prosthetic), 72021 (X-Ray).

The health care professional may give you more than one diagnosis code or procedure code.

---

Do you file for authorization/precertification?

Will you submit my claim to my insurance company?

Will you help file appeals or will you appeal if a service is denied coverage?

Do you accept discounts from the insurance company?

Do I have to pay up front?

What is your refund process or how long will it take to get a refund?

---

**I WANT MY MONEY!**

Some health care professionals require you to pay before they bill your health insurance plan. For instance, some hospitals want you to pay them your deductible before the surgery. But when you get your **EOB**, you find out you don't owe the amount you paid the hospital. Guess what? They owe you a refund!

---

Do you offer discounts or some form of financial assistance for the medical bill?

Can you place my account on a 30 day hold while my insurance company adjusts my claim?

*If you are having surgery...*

Will any other healthcare professionals be assisting during the surgery?   If so what are their names and how will they be assisting?   Are they anesthesiologists, assistant surgeons?

What facility will the procedure be done at?

## DID YOU KNOW?

If you have surgery, every health care professional that is involved will send a bill to your insurance company. That's a bill from the hospital, the surgeon, the anesthesiologist, the assistant surgeon, the pathologist, etc.

Do you send my lab work to another health care professional for testing? If so, Can you send my lab work to my in-network lab?

## DID YOU KNOW?

You can ask your doctor to send your labs to specific facilities – that way you can make sure your lab work will be sent to an in network facility.

*If your doctor's office is in a hospital...*

Will the hospital bill my insurance for the use of the facility during an office visit?

What name does the facility bill under?

What is the billing tax id number and billing address?

# IN-NETWORK OR OUT-OF-NETWORK

To answer this question most assume you ask the doctor or facility. But the health care professional may have contracts with several different insurance companies, they may even take your insurance, but that doesn't mean they are in your network.

Let's assume you have ABC Insurance and you ask the doctor's office – "Are you in-network with my insurance?" The most likely response is, "Yes, we take ABC." But that doesn't mean the doctor is in-network sometimes that just means that they will file your claim for you.

Ask your health care professional for their **tax id number (TIN)** which is a 9 digit identifier – usually in the format 12-3456789 – and their billing address to find out if they are in-network with your insurance plan.

# Things to ask my insurance company

Is this health care professional in-network?

Is this procedure covered by my insurance? Are there any criteria that need to be met before it is covered by insurance? Can I have a copy of the requirements for this treatment to be covered?

## IS IT COVERED?

Sometimes you need to know if a certain test or procedure your doctor wants you to have is actually covered by your insurance plan or if it requires authorization. To find out you need the **diagnosis code** and the **procedure code** from the health care professional.

Does this procedure need authorization – how long does this take. How will I be notified of the decision? If authorization is denied what are the next steps to get an approval?

Are there any visit limits for a certain type of procedure? How many times can I go to physical therapy, a chiropractor, etc. per plan year?

Does my plan have pre-existing condition limitations?

Is there an annual maximum or lifetime maximum for my plan or for certain benefits?

Is my plan a contract year or calendar year?

Does my plan have any carry over months?

---

**CARRY OVER MONTHS**

Any allowed medical expenses that applied to your deductible during the last 3 months of your plan year will be applied to the deductible for the next plan year. Your health plan may not offer carry over months.

---

If my doctor is out-of-network can I get an authorization for him to be treated as in-network?

What in network labs should my doctor send my lab work to?

Can I get a list of doctors, hospitals, labs that are in network in my area?

How long does my health care professional have to send in claims?

How long do I have to request an adjustment?

How do I file appeals? How long does it take for a decision?

# When in Doubt

This book has presented the basics of how health insurance works. If there are questions that you have about your insurance plan or more information that you want about how your coverage works, contact your health insurance plan.

Made in United States
North Haven, CT
06 July 2023

38628833R00046